BIOGRAPHY FROM ANCIENT CIVILIZATIONS

LEGENDS, FOLKLORE, AND STORIES OF ANCIENT WORLDS

The Life and Times of

THUCYDIDES

Mitchell Lane
PUBLISHERS

P.O. Box 196
Hockessin, Delaware 19707
www.mitchelllane.com

TITLES IN THE SERIES

The Life and Times of

BIOGRAPHY FROM ANCIENT CIVILIZATIONS

LEGENDS, FOLKLORE, AND STORIES OF ANCIENT WORLDS

The Life and Times of

THUCYDIDES

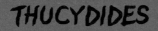

Jim Whiting

Mitchell Lane PUBLISHERS

Copyright © 2009 by Mitchell Lane Publishers, Inc. All rights reserved. No part of this book may be reproduced without written permission from the publisher. Printed and bound in the United States of America.

Printing   1   2   3   4   5   6   7   8   9

Library of Congress Cataloging-in-Publication Data

Whiting, Jim, 1943–
  The life and times of Thucydides / by Jim Whiting.
      p. cm. — (Biography from ancient civilizations)
  Includes bibliographical references and index.
  ISBN 978-1-58415-698-7 (library bound)
  1. Thucydides—Juvenile literature. 2. Thucydides. History of the Peloponnesian War—Juvenile literature. 3. Greece—History—Peloponnesian War, 431–404 B.C.—Historiography—Juvenile literature. 4. Historians—Greece—Biography—Juvenile literature. I. Title.
  DF229.T6W5 2009
  938'.05072—dc22

                                                                        2008020923

ABOUT THE AUTHOR: Jim Whiting has been a remarkably versatile and accomplished journalist, writer, and photographer for more than thirty years. He has written dozens of children's books, including *The Life and Times of Plato*, *The Life and Times of Pericles*, *The Life and Times of Nero*, and *The Life and Times of Hippocrates* for Mitchell Lane Publishers. He and his wife live in Washington State.

PUBLISHER'S NOTE: This story is based on the author's extensive research, which he believes to be accurate. Documentation of such research is contained on page 46.

The internet sites referenced herein were active as of the publication date. Due to the fleeting nature of some web sites, we cannot guarantee they will all be active when you are reading this book.

To reflect current usage, we have chosen to use the secular era designations BCE ("before the common era") and CE ("of the common era") instead of the traditional designations BC ("before Christ") and AD (*anno Domini*, "in the year of the Lord").

                                                                        PLB

BIOGRAPHY FROM ANCIENT CIVILIZATIONS
LEGENDS, FOLKLORE, AND STORIES OF ANCIENT WORLDS

CONTENTS

*For Your Information

Soldiers from the Greek colony of Syracuse on the island of Sicily attack the Athenian army. The Athenians had invaded two years earlier but were unable to secure a victory.

CHAPTER
ONE

SURRENDER AT SYRACUSE

The Assinarus River was the last shred of hope for the thousands of desperate men. They were the remnants of an Athenian army that had landed on the island of Sicily in 415 BCE, just two years earlier. They had expected an easy conquest of Syracuse, one of the largest settlements on the island.

Syracuse had been settled by their fellow Greeks many years earlier, but the Peloponnesian War—which pitted Greek against Greek—had been raging for nearly twenty years. The Athenians confidently believed that this invasion would become a major step in finally ending the war, and ending it in their favor. But a series of disastrous decisions—and an untimely assist or two from the natural world—had shattered this belief. No longer was there any chance of conquering Syracuse. Now all the Athenians wanted to do was escape with their lives.

They had been on the run for a week and become little more than a disorganized, discouraged rabble. Their enemies seemed to be on all sides of them, launching attacks that killed men every day. They were exhausted, desperately hungry, and above all suffering from almost unbearable thirst in the hot early autumn sun. When the men saw the Assinarus River, most of them broke ranks and plunged into the water.

"Once there they rushed in, and all order was at an end, each man wanting to cross first, and the attacks of the enemy making it difficult to cross at all; forced to huddle together, they fell against and trampled one another, some dying immediately upon the javelins, others getting entangled together and stumbling over the articles of baggage, without being able to rise again,"[1] wrote the man who left behind the best description of the impending catastrophe.

The ground on the far side of the river was elevated. Their enemies took advantage of the heights to rain arrows and spears onto them. Hundreds collapsed and died in the river.

The account continues, "The [enemies] also came down and butchered them, especially those in the water, which was thus immediately spoiled, but which they went on drinking just the same, mud and all, bloody as it was, most even fighting to have it."[2]

With the situation turning hopeless, the Athenian commander surrendered. Their suffering was far from over. Many of the captured soldiers were sent into the stone quarries near Syracuse. Given little food or water and no sanitary facilities, nearly all were literally worked to death.

The ruins of ancient stone quarries in Syracuse. Athenian prisoners were forced to mine stone for Syracusean building projects.

It was an ignominious end to a campaign that had begun with high hopes. An estimated 40,000 men had left Athens. Only a handful ever returned to their homes and their families.

The account of this disaster comes from an Athenian author named Thucydides (thoo-SID-ih-deez). His book *History of the Peloponnesian War* is one of the most studied works of the ancient era.

The title is derived from the location of Sparta, which was on the Peloponnesian (peh-leh-puh-NEE-zhun) peninsula in Greece. Its inhabitants, along with the Athenians, were the primary combatants of the war.

The book goes into great detail about the course of most of the war, which changed the boundaries and powers of the ancient world. Thucydides viewed the battle for Syracuse and its aftermath as the most important section of his book.

"This was the greatest Hellenic [Greek] achievement of any in this war, or, in my opinion, in Hellenic history; at once glorious to the victors, and most calamitous to the conquered," he wrote. "They were beaten at all points and altogether; all that they suffered was great; they were destroyed, as the saying is, with a total destruction, their fleet, their army—everything was destroyed, and few out of many returned home."[3]

Thucydides was in a unique position to write about the war. "I lived through the whole of it, being of an age to comprehend events, and giving my attention to them in order to know the exact truth about them,"[4] he noted. He had also been a general in the Athenian army about a decade earlier. As a result, he had firsthand experience with wartime tactics and strategies.

However, it was his misfortune to be in command during an Athenian military defeat. His fellow Athenians blamed him for the loss and voted to send him into exile. For his purposes, it turned out to be a blessing.

"It was also my fate to be an exile from my country for twenty years after my command," he continued. "Being present with both parties, and more especially with the Peloponnesians by reason of my exile, I had leisure to observe affairs more closely."[5]

"Observing affairs more closely" didn't extend to his personal life. In spite of the amount of detail that Thucydides provides in his chronicle

A bust of Thucydides, Louvre, Paris

of the war, he remains a shadowy figure. He mentions himself only a few times.

Because of his reputation and fame, several writers who came later—sometimes centuries later—added more clues. Most of this information cannot be verified. Consequently, educated guesses are about as close as historians can come to piecing together his life.

Almost certainly he was born in the Greek region of Thrace, located northeast of Athens. His most likely birth date is sometime between 460 and 455 BCE. His father was Olorus, a prominent nobleman of the region. Thucydides was related by marriage to several important Athenians. One was Miltiades, the hero of the Athenian victory over an invading Persian army at the Battle of Marathon in 490. Another was Miltiades' son Cimon, an important Athenian general for several decades.

One of the very few personal details Thucydides reveals is that he "possessed the right of working the gold mines in [Thasos, an island a few miles off the coast of Thrace] and had thus great influence with the inhabitants of the mainland."[6] As a result, he was particularly well-to-do. He would have had the opportunity for the best possible education and learning from the best minds of the era.

At some point he moved to Athens and eventually regarded himself as a citizen of the city. He probably also maintained a residence in Thrace.

It is not clear when he began writing *History of the Peloponnesian War*. Some historians believe that he waited until the end of the war in 404. At that point, his exile may have been lifted, allowing him to return to Athens. Others maintain that he started writing it much sooner.

He didn't complete the work. It breaks off, almost in mid-sentence, as he discusses events that occurred in 411. The war would last for seven more years. The most likely explanation for this abrupt ending is that he died at that point.

As is the case with almost all of his life, the circumstances of his death and its timing are shrouded in mystery. The most widely accepted dates of his death range between 400 and 397 BCE. According to the Roman historian Plutarch (who was writing in the first century CE, nearly

Athenian and Spartan soldiers clash on an ancient Greek vase that shows a battle from the Peloponnesian War.

An ancient mosaic shows Thucydides wreathed in laurel leaves, the highest prize in literature in ancient Greece.

500 years later), he came to an untimely end: "It is said, too, that Thucydides was murdered at Skapte Hyle, a place in Thrace."[7] There is no way to verify this assertion. Plutarch is on firmer ground in another respect: "His monument is to be seen among those of Cimon's family near the tomb of Cimon's sister, Elpinice."[8]

While his burial monument has long since disappeared, the *History of the Peloponnesian War* endures as a monumental masterpiece for its author.

The Rise of Athens

The settlement of Athens dates from at least three thousand years ago. Early in the sixth century BCE, it began emerging as one of the most prosperous Greek poleis. One major reason was a series of reforms instituted by the Athenian leader Solon. These reforms helped close the gap between rich and poor people.

In 561, Peisistratus (py-SIS-truh-tus) took control of the city. Though he was a dictator, he ruled for the benefit of most of the people. His son Hippias (hih-PEE-us) wasn't as successful and was overthrown in 510. Three years later, under the leadership of Cleisthenes (KLYS-thuh-neez), all Athenian citizens were given the right to vote.

At first, citizenship was limited to males with an Athenian parent. Later this requirement was tightened even further, requiring both parents to be Athenians. The rest of the people in Athens—foreigners, slaves, and women—were not counted as citizens, and therefore could not vote.

In spite of those limitations on voting, most historians regard Athens as the birthplace of democracy. Ancient Greek historian Herodotus certainly felt that way. He described the Persian Wars at the start of the fifth century BCE, in which Athens played a key role in the struggle against the Persian invaders. An outnumbered Athenian army won a stunning victory at the Battle of Marathon in 490, then led a coalition of Greek poleis in a victorious naval battle at Salamis ten years later.

The Parthenon on the Acropolis in ancient Athens

"Athens went from strength to strength, and proved, if proof was needed, how noble a thing equality before the law is, not in one respect only, but in all; for while they were oppressed under tyrants, they had no better success in war than any of their neighbors, yet, once the yoke was flung off, they proved the finest fighters in the world," Herodotus wrote. "This clearly shows that, as long as they were held down by authority, they deliberately shirked their duty in the field, as slaves shirk working for their masters; but when freedom was won, then every man amongst them was interested in his own cause."[9]

Heavily armed Athenian soldiers rout the invading Persians at the Battle of Marathon. More than 6,000 Persians were killed, while just 192 Athenians died.

CHAPTER
TWO

THE PRELUDE TO WAR

Writing in the third person, Thucydides began his book, "Thucydides, an Athenian, wrote the history of the war between the Peloponnesians and the Athenians, beginning at the moment that it broke out, and believing that it would be a great war, and more worthy of relation than any that had preceded it."[1]

He was primarily referring to two earlier conflicts as well as their authors. One was the Trojan War, most notably chronicled by the great poet Homer in his classic works *The Iliad* and *The Odyssey*. Among Greeks, Homer had an exalted status. Students had to memorize long passages of his poems.

The other was *The Persian War*. Its author, Herodotus (her-AH-duh-tus), is usually regarded as the first person to write history. He had been very popular during his life. Large crowds attended public readings of his works.

Thucydides wasn't shy about taking them on. He referred directly to them when he wrote, "The conclusions I have drawn from the proofs quoted may, I believe, safely be relied upon. Assuredly they will not be disturbed either by the verses of a poet displaying the exaggeration of his craft, or by the compositions of the chroniclers that are attractive at truth's expense."[2]

As classics professor Leo Strauss points out, "[Thucydides] engages in a contest with Homer. Homer lived long after the Trojan War; this alone makes him a questionable witness to the Trojan War. Above all, Homer is a poet. Poets magnify and adorn and they tell fabulous stories; they thus conceal the truth about human beings and human nature."[3]

By contrast, Strauss continues, Thucydides "reveals the character of human life by presenting deeds and speeches which are not magnified and adorned."[4]

Unlike Homer, Herodotus had been born shortly before the Persian invasion. When he wrote his book, he interviewed men who had been involved in the actual fighting.

Herodotus apparently recorded almost everything he heard, and some of the stories are truly incredible. For example, he wrote about a race of giant ants that attacked men and killed them. As noted historian Victor Davis Hanson observes, "[Herodotus] feels no need to assess—at least not in any systematic or formal way—the accuracy of what he hears, and provides little idea how all these reports join and fit into a unified whole."[5]

On the other hand, Hanson says that Thucydides "believes that the truth requires his own interpretation of the events he presents. It demands that he deem some occurrences not worthy of inclusion into his narrative, while others must take on unusual importance."[6]

There is one other vital difference between Thucydides and his predecessors. Thucydides was interested only in human nature and how it affected the course of the war. In his reports, the gods didn't interfere in human affairs. His account is entirely naturalistic.

Though the war began in 431, its origins could be traced back by many years. People throughout ancient Greece had several things in common—most notably language, culture, and religion, plus they met every four years for the Olympic Games. However, they didn't think of themselves as citizens of a country called Greece. Rather, the ancient Greek landscape was dotted with hundreds of poleis (POH-lays), or city-states. Each polis (POH-lis) consisted of a central town or city and the surrounding countryside. Conflicts between poleis were common.

Many of the poleis came together in 480 to defeat a massive Persian army that invaded Greece in an effort to add the Greeks to the Persian Empire. Almost as soon as the Persian threat was eliminated, they went back to their incessant bickering. Athens and Sparta emerged as the two dominant Greek poleis. Many of the other poleis allied themselves with one of these two.

The victory over the Persians was especially meaningful for Athens. It allowed the democracy that had begun a few decades earlier to develop. Under the leadership of the statesman Pericles (PAYR-ih-kleez), Athens entered what historians call the Golden Age of Greece. Art, architecture, drama, medicine, and philosophy all flourished. The city's most famous monuments date from this era. The centerpiece was the Parthenon, a temple built to the goddess of wisdom, Athena. The temple still stands and draws countless visitors from all over the world.

Many other Greeks didn't welcome this development. They felt that Athens was becoming too powerful. The city became almost dictatorial in its approach, even to its allies.

This concern was especially apparent in Sparta. Increasing tensions led to open warfare between the two sides in 460, in what many historians call the First Peloponnesian War. (In general, however, when historians refer to the Peloponnesian War, they are referring to the events that Thucydides chronicles). The conflict lasted for fifteen years but settled little. In 445, the Thirty Years' Treaty ended the fighting. It didn't end the underlying problems.

The event that set off the Peloponnesian War occurred in the remote Greek colony of Epidamnus (eh-puh-DAHM-nuss), hundreds of miles from Athens. Thucydides let his readers know where it was: "The city of Epidamnus stands on the right of the entrance of the Ionian gulf."[7]

In 436, the citizens overthrew the aristocrats who had ruled the city for many years and established a democratic government. The aristocrats weren't about to give up their position without a fight. They got support from Illyria, a nearby kingdom, and attacked the city.

Many years earlier, Epidamnus had been founded by the people of Corcyra (kor-SY-ruh, modern-day Corfu). The besieged democrats in Epidamnus appealed to Corcyra for help. The Corcyrans ignored them.

Corcyra had been established by Corinth, a major polis. In spite of their common heritage, Corinth and Corcyra had been enemies for many years. In desperation, the Epidamnians appealed to Corinth. The Corinthians sent soldiers and settlers to their aid.

Corinthian leaders knew that their decision would create tension with their former colony. It's not clear why they made this decision, because there wasn't any practical reason for them to become involved. Thucydides offers a possible explanation: The Corinthians "hated the Corcyrans for their contempt of the mother country. Instead of meeting with the usual honors accorded to the parent city by every other colony at public assemblies, such as precedence at sacrifices, Corinth found herself treated with contempt."[8] In other words, Corcyra disrespected Corinth.

The Corcyrans quickly reacted. At that time, they had one of the largest and more powerful navies in the Greek world. They sent part of their fleet to Epidamnus. The intervention proved decisive. The democrats surrendered. The aristocrats resumed power and kicked out the Corinthian settlers who had just arrived.

The Corinthians burned for revenge and spent two years building up their navy. Corinth was also part of the Peloponnesian League, headed by Sparta and including numerous poleis. Aware of the impending threat from Corinth and perhaps other poleis, the Corcyrans appealed to Athens for help.

What at first seemed a relatively minor dispute over an obscure polis now threatened to involve the Greek superpowers. The Corcyrans knew Athens would have little interest in a quarrel many miles away, so they appealed to the Athenians' sense of fear. They said that the Spartans and their allies wanted to start a war against Athens, and that when this happened, Athens would need all the allies it could get—especially Corcyra with its large fleet. After a long debate, the Athenians voted in favor of the alliance. However, they sent only ten ships to help the Corcyrans. This was just a small fraction of their massive fleet, by far the largest in the ancient Greek world and the major source of Athenian power and influence.

According to historian Donald Kagan, this was a "policy of minimal deterrence."[9] The hope was that these ships would show that Athens meant business, while the small number would indicate that they didn't mean to challenge Corinth. Ideally, the Corinthians would simply choose not to fight and the crisis would pass.

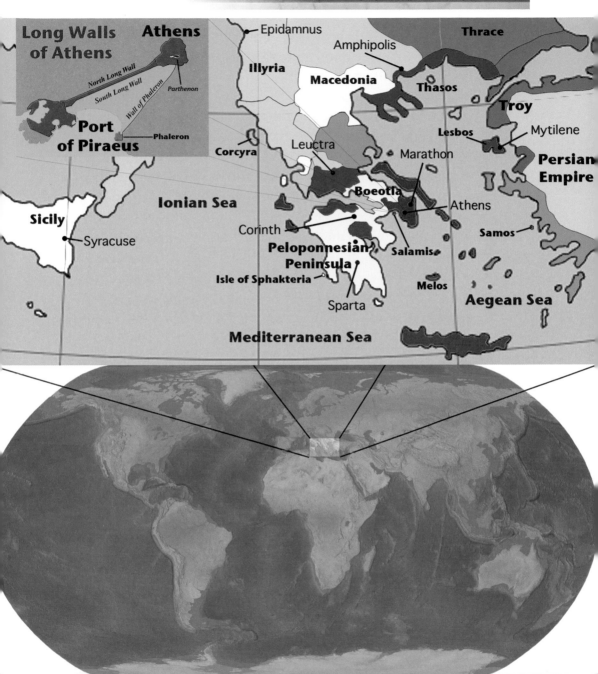

Sparta and Athens were the two main combatants in the Peloponnesian War. The yellow areas show Sparta and its allies; red shows Athens and its allies; and dark blue shows neutral poleis. Inset: The Long Walls linked Athens and the Port of Piraeus, allowing the city to be continually supplied by sea.

It didn't. The Corinthians attacked the Corcyran fleet and were on the verge of victory when twenty more Athenian ships appeared. The Corinthians broke off the fight.

The Corinthians were furious at the Athenian intervention. They were determined to enlist the rest of the Peloponnesian League in their quarrel. Several other incidents increased the tension.

Up to this point, the Spartans had remained on the sidelines. With Athens having appeared to attack one of the most important members in the Peloponnesian League, they felt obligated to react. Accordingly, they summoned a league conference in 432 BCE. It was inconclusive until the Corinthian delegation made their case. They said that if the Spartans wouldn't stand with them, they would withdraw from the league and seek support elsewhere. That sealed the deal. Even the suggestion of leaving was very upsetting to the Spartans. The league voted for war.

In an effort to avoid a confrontation, the Spartans made several peace overtures to Athens. None succeeded. The most likely reason is that Pericles didn't want peace. He probably believed that war between the two Greek superpowers was inevitable, and that Athens would win. Such a victory would make Athens even more powerful and finally end the long-simmering tensions with its rival.

With their huge fleet, the Athenians were dominant at sea. The Spartans were dominant on land. But the Spartans couldn't use their land dominance to attack Athens directly. The city was invulnerable because of the Long Walls, a series of fortifications that completely surrounded it and extended for several miles to the port city of Piraeus. Its superiority at sea guaranteed that it could continue to import the grain and other food it needed to survive indefinitely. In all likelihood, Pericles believed that Athens would outlast Sparta. It would win by not losing.

As historian A.R. Burn notes, "Sparta would presently have to give up the struggle, with disastrous loss of 'face'; it would be made clear that she could not defend her naval allies. They would have to come to terms with Athens."[10]

In 431, the fighting began. It would last for twenty-seven years and forever alter the Greek landscape.

Sparta

Ancient Sparta produced the finest soldiers in Greece. From the Spartans' point of view, this was essential for their survival as a society. Their way of life was founded on the virtual enslavement of their neighbors, who were known as Helots. The Helots did all the grunt work, primarily working on farms and in Spartan homes. Because the Helots vastly outnumbered their masters, the Spartans always had to be on their guard against revolts and viciously suppressed them whenever they started. In addition, the Spartans faced threats from other poleis.

Almost every male in Sparta trained rigorously for the military. A boy's training began literally at birth. Babies were closely examined. If they showed any signs of defects, they were taken outside and left to die.

At the age of seven, boys were taken away from their mothers and sent to live in military barracks. These barracks became their homes for many years. As a matter of policy, the conditions were harsh. Meals usually consisted of black broth and wine. Youngsters were encouraged to steal food, but they were beaten if caught. On the few occasions when they took baths, the water was ice cold. (Today the word *spartan* is used to describe living conditions that are very plain, without any luxuries.)

Above all, Spartan boys learned how to fight—and fight as disciplined members of the army. According to a commonly accepted saying, a Spartan soldier was expected to return home after battle—with his shield or on it (dead).

Because the men were constantly training, Spartan women were among the freest and most fit of the ancient Greek women. The Spartans realized that healthy mothers produced healthy children, so they educated their women and made sure they ate well. Above all, as Plutarch points out, women exercised "themselves with wrestling, running, throwing the quoit and casting the dart, to the end that the fruit [babies] they conceived might, in strong and healthy bodies, take firmer root and find better growth."[11]

They also married later in life and were therefore less likely to die during pregnancy or childbirth. Many even became wealthy.

Statue of a Spartan Hoplite, 5th century BCE

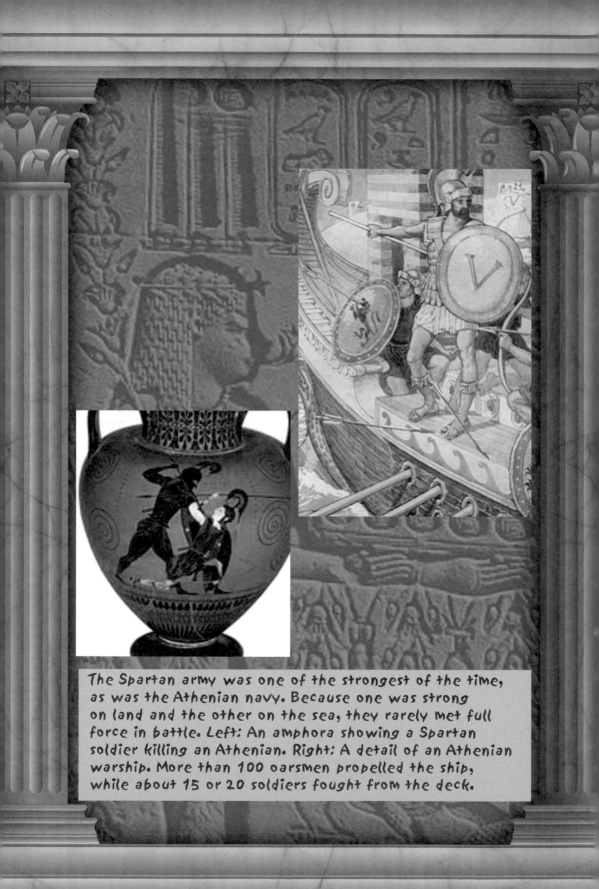

The Spartan army was one of the strongest of the time, as was the Athenian navy. Because one was strong on land and the other on the sea, they rarely met full force in battle. Left: An amphora showing a Spartan soldier killing an Athenian. Right: A detail of an Athenian warship. More than 100 oarsmen propelled the ship, while about 15 or 20 soldiers fought from the deck.

CHAPTER
THREE

THE ELEPHANT AND THE WHALE

The Spartans prepared to march, though their commander Archidamus (ar-kuh-DAH-mus) opposed war. He sent an envoy to Athens to offer one final opportunity to negotiate peace. It did no good. Pericles had issued orders that no Spartan was allowed into the city.

"Both sides nourished the boldest hopes and put forth their utmost strength for the war," Thucydides wrote. "The Peloponnesus and Athens were both full of young men whose inexperience made them eager to take up arms, while the rest of Hellas [Greece] stood straining with excitement at the conflict of its leading cities."[1]

The Spartans took advantage of their superiority to storm into Attica, the region of which Athens was the center. While many Athenians urged Pericles to confront the invaders, he refused. Instead, he ordered the people living in the countryside to take refuge in the city. When the Spartans burned their farms, most of the citizens were safely inside the city walls.

The Spartans could not stay in Attica indefinitely. After they departed, the Athenians used their fleet to raid the Peloponnesian coast. Once again there were not many casualties. As Sir Nigel Bagnall, a retired British army general, points out, "There was a stalemate—an elephant versus a whale—with neither of the protagonists being able to bring about a decisive encounter."[2]

When campaigning ended that year, Pericles delivered one of the most famous speeches in history, which said, in part:

Athens alone of her contemporaries is found when tested to be greater than her reputation. Such is the Athens for which these men, in the assertion of their resolve not to lose her, nobly fought and died; and well may every one of their survivors be ready to suffer in her cause.[3]

Called the Funeral Oration, it influenced the speeches delivered after the Battle of Gettysburg in 1863 during the Civil War, including President Abraham Lincoln's. "Like Lincoln, Pericles' intention was to explain to the living in the midst of a difficult war why their sufferings were justified and why their continued dedication was necessary," historian Donald Kagan observes. "In the process he painted the most glorious and attractive picture we have of the character of the Athenian democracy and its superiority to the Spartan way of life."[4]

Pericles gives his Funeral Oration below the Acropolis.

Neither Pericles nor anyone listening to him had any idea of the suffering that was about to befall them. The second year of the war began with Sparta once again invading Attica and the Athenians once again retreating to the safety of the city. While the Spartans couldn't get inside the Long Walls, another enemy could—ironically, through the port of Piraeus, which served as the city's lifeline to the outside world. Sometime in 430 BCE, a ship bringing food was also carrying a plague. The disease quickly roared through Athens.

"People in good health were all of a sudden attacked by violent heats in the head, and redness and inflammation in the eyes, the inward parts, such as the throat or tongue, becoming bloody and emitting an unnatural and fetid breath," Thucydides wrote. "It burned so that the patient could not bear to have on him clothing or linen even of the very lightest description."[5]

Thucydides spoke from firsthand experience. According to one of his few biographical details, "I had the disease myself, and watched its operation in the case of others."[6]

After days of agony, many victims died. The number of bodies soon overwhelmed the survivors, who could no longer bury them properly. According to estimates, at least one fourth of the population perished.

The most prominent victim was Pericles himself. Thucydides admired Pericles, saying, "Pericles indeed, by his rank, ability, and known integrity, was enabled to exercise an independent control over the multitude—in short, to lead them instead of being led by them."[7]

When he died, leadership was passed to men who didn't have all these qualities. This void would eventually prove tragic for Athens.

Somehow the city managed to overcome its grievous losses and continue the war, but part of the noble character that Pericles had praised seemed to have been lost. In 428 BCE the polis of Mytilene (mih-tih-LEE-nee) on the island of Lesbos revolted. The uprising was quickly put down, and the Athenians voted to kill all the men in Mytilene and sell the women and children into slavery. They sent a ship to tell the Athenian troops at Mytilene to carry out that decision. The next day they changed their minds and dispatched another ship with new orders to spare the inhabitants. The desperate men in the second ship rowed in relays and arrived just in time to prevent the harsh sentence from being carried out.

In spite of the respite, the original order showed how the feelings of the people had changed. As the future would reveal, similar events would not inspire acts of mercy.

The war dragged on. The possibility of a breakthrough came in 425. The Athenians trapped a Spartan force on the island of Sphakteria (sfak-tuh-REE-uh). After losing nearly a third of their men, the Spartans surrendered. A Spartan surrender was almost unprecedented, and the shockwaves reverberated throughout Greece.

To regain their imprisoned comrades, the Spartans offered peace. Puffed up after defeating the seemingly invincible Spartans, the Athenians demanded some territory. The Spartans refused, so their soldiers remained in Athenian hands and the war continued.

The captured Spartans had immense value. The Athenians made it clear that they would be executed the moment a Spartan army entered Attica. This respite from invasion led to further Athenian optimism. In 424 BCE, an Athenian army invaded Boeotia (bee-OH-shuh), a major Spartan ally located north of Athens.

The two sides met at Delium for the first major battle of the war. At first the Athenians enjoyed success, pushing back part of the Boeotian line. But a counterattack routed the Athenians and sent them into a headlong flight.

The battle had two notable outcomes. One was the heroism of a young Athenian cavalryman named Alcibiades (al-sih-BY-uh-deez). A member of one of Athens' most prominent families, Alcibiades used the reports of his valor to begin a meteoric rise in military rank. Less than a decade later he would use his exalted position to help lead the disaster at Syracuse. The other notable outcome was the survival of Socrates, a teacher in Athens. His ideas and his students would have a major influence on the course of Western civilization.

Later in 424, Athens was rocked by another setback. Led by Brasidas (bruh-SEE-dus), a Spartan army attacked the city of Amphipolis (am-FIH-puh-lus) in Thrace. The Athenian commander in the city, Eucles (YOO-kleez), sent a desperate message to Thucydides asking for help. By then a general, Thucydides commanded the Athenian fleet in the region. However, he was more than 50 miles away on the island of Thasos and couldn't provide immediate aid. That delay would prove costly.

Brasidas offered moderate terms to the city's inhabitants if they surrendered immediately. They accepted. Thucydides arrived to find the city in the hands of Brasidas' troops.

The Athenians blamed Thucydides for the city's loss and put him on trial. He was found guilty and exiled. Characteristically, Thucydides barely mentions this pivotal personal event and makes no effort to defend himself.

The inconclusive fighting continued. With no apparent end in sight, in 421 the two sides agreed to halt the fighting. Called the Peace of Nicias (NISH-ee-us) after the Athenian leader who helped bring it about, it was supposed to last for fifty years. In reality, it would last barely five.

Pericles' Funeral Oration and the Gettysburg Address

Most people can instantly identify "Fourscore and seven years ago" as the beginning of Abraham Lincoln's Gettysburg Address. Lincoln delivered it at burial ceremonies for Union soldiers after the bloody Civil War battle of Gettysburg.

Historian Garry Wills compares the ceremonies at Gettysburg with Pericles' Funeral Oration. He suggests that Lincoln may have modeled his speech after Pericles'.

Civil War historian James McPherson points out that both Lincoln's and Pericles' speeches used contrast as illustration. One of these contrasts is the difference between teachers and those whom they teach. He compares Thucydides' words: "By their deaths, those who fell in the war with Sparta taught the polis to live," with Lincoln's: "From these honored dead we take increased devotion to that cause for which they gave the last full measure of devotion."[8]

Other historians disagree. They say Lincoln's primary literary influences came from the Bible and from Shakespeare.

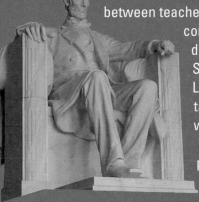

Lincoln Memorial, Washington, D.C.

There is no doubt about Pericles' influence on the day's primary speaker, Edward Everett. A noted orator, Everett addressed the crowd for nearly two hours, and he constantly referred to Athens, the Battle of Marathon, Greek drama, and other aspects of Greek culture. He was very familiar with Thucydides and Pericles.

Some of his knowledge came from firsthand experience. According to Wills, Everett "went to Greece, to walk over the battlefields where the first democracy of the West won its freedom. He returned to America convinced that a new Athens was rising here."[9]

At Gettysburg, Wills says, Everett "opened his speech with a detailed description of the annual funeral rite at which Pericles had spoken, comparing it point for point with the ceremony for the Union dead."[10] The rest of the speech continually referred to Pericles and the Athenians. Wills writes that Everett's intention was to "use Greek ideals to express America to Americans."[11]

In the end, Americans didn't catch on. Everett's speech has largely been forgotten. To Wills, Everett's flaw was that he only looked backward. By contrast, Wills notes, "It was the challenge *of the moment* that both Pericles and Lincoln addressed."[12] That is why their words continue to ring true.

A museum display of bronze helmets dating from the time of the Peloponnesian War. The helmets were heavy and hot. Soldiers usually waited until just before battle to put them on.

CHAPTER
FOUR

THE COST OF OVERCONFIDENCE

To many, the Peace of Nicias seemed to favor Athens. Spartans suffered because the hostages remained in Athenian hands, and because of reverses that included the loss of Brasidas and other generals. They "scarcely dared to take the field, but fancied that they could not stir without a blunder, for being new to the experience of adversity they had lost all confidence in themselves,"[1] Thucydides wrote.

Victor Davis Hanson observes, "Pericles' vision, though tattered and torn, seemed fulfilled. Contemporaries in 421 thought Sparta was checked and demoralized."[2]

Some Athenians weren't satisfied with the treaty. Its most notable opponent was Alcibiades, who had a very high opinion of himself. He was "offended with the Spartans for having negotiated the treaty through Nicias and Laches [LAY-keez; another Athenian leader], and for having overlooked him on account of his youth,"[3] Thucydides reports.

Thucydides didn't think much of Alcibiades. "Although in his public life his conduct of the war was as good as could be desired, in his private life his habits gave offense to everyone,"[4] he wrote. Alcibiades' actions over the following years would support Thucydides' opinion on both counts.

The Peace of Nicias was fragile because neither side trusted the other. In addition, some of the major poleis refused to accept it. Fueling the distrust, Alcibiades began scheming with several poleis in the

Peloponnese to undermine Sparta. Not only did these poleis pose direct military threats to Sparta, they were also in a position to encourage the ultimate Spartan nightmare: a successful revolt by the Helots, who heavily outnumbered their Spartan masters and were the underpinning of Sparta's economy.

This situation came to a head in 418. The Spartans won an overwhelming victory at the battle of Mantinea (man-tuh-NEE-uh). It brought several poleis under their control and restored their confidence in battle.

Although some Athenian soldiers had fought against the Spartans, the two armies maintained their uneasy peace. Nevertheless, the Greek landscape remained a very dangerous place. As Thucydides commented, The Peace of Nicias "cannot, it will be found, be rationally considered a state of peace, as neither party either gave or got back all that they had agreed."[5]

In 416, the Athenians invaded the island of Melos and captured it after a long siege. The Athenians "put to death all the grown men whom they took, and sold the women and children for slaves, and subsequently sent five hundred colonists and settled the place themselves,"[6] Thucydides noted. To Plutarch, the atrocity rested largely with Alcibiades: "He was the principal cause of the slaughter,"[7] he wrote.

Regardless of responsibility, the way that Thucydides organized his book suggests that in his opinion this deterioration of the character of the Athenians was at least partly responsible for the disaster at Syracuse. Immediately after describing the dismal fate of the Melians, he writes: "The same winter the Athenians resolved to sail again to Sicily . . . to conquer the island; most of them being ignorant of its size and of the number of its inhabitants, Hellenic and barbarian, and of the fact that they were undertaking a war not much inferior to that against the Peloponnesians."[8]

Once again the Athenians were drawn into a quarrel that arose far from home. This one began with Segesta, a colony in Sicily with which they had a loose alliance. The Segestans started a war with a neighboring colony, which enlisted help from Syracuse. Segesta asked Athens to intervene on its behalf and offered some support. Like the Corcyrans,

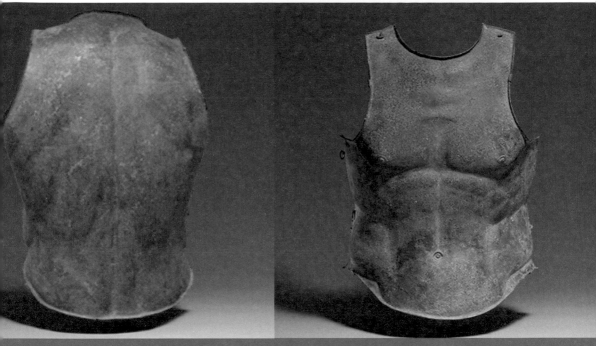

The backplate (left) and chestplate of bronze body armor from the fourth century BCE, on display at the Metropolitan Museum of Art in New York City. The armor offered protection from weapons but hampered movement.

they also appealed to fear: If Segesta fell, Syracuse would go on to conquer all of Sicily, then join Sparta and try to conquer Athens.

Nicias argued against the expedition, but he was bettered by Alcibiades, who told his fellow citizens that the Syracusans were not very good soldiers and predicted an easy Athenian victory. Above all, he emphasized, "We have reached a position in which we must not be content with retaining what we have but must scheme to extend it."[9]

According to Thucydides, Pericles was most missed at this moment. When he was alive, Pericles urged his fellow citizens "to wait quietly, to pay attention to their marine [navy], to attempt no new conquests, and to expose the city to no new hazards during the war, and doing this, promised them a favorable result."[10]

Pericles had been dead for more than a decade. Memories of his moderate approach had faded. Goaded by Alcibiades, the Athenians authorized a huge fleet and thousands of men to undertake the invasion. On the eve of departure, someone defaced statues of the god Hermes

A statue of the Greek god Hermes holding the infant Dionysus (the god of wine). Statues of Hermes were defaced just before the Athenian fleet sailed. Although Hermes is best known as the messenger of the gods, he also served as the god of travelers.

throughout Athens. To the Athenians, it was a bad omen, but the fleet sailed anyway. They still expected an easy victory.

Almost from the start, the expedition ran into problems. Segesta provided far fewer resources than it had promised. Rather than launch an immediate attack against Syracuse, the Athenians did virtually nothing for several months. In addition, Alcibiades, who had sailed to Syracuse, was ordered to return to Athens to face trial for defacing the statues and other offenses. In spite of his popularity, his arrogance and obvious ambition had created many enemies. Fearing the possible outcome, he escaped and fled to Sparta. The trial went forward without him, and he was sentenced to die.

The following spring, the Athenians, under the command of Nicias, finally launched an offensive. The Syracusans, given so many months to prepare, fought back with determination. The Athenians slowly gained the upper hand, but Nicias couldn't achieve a decisive victory.

The Athenians were running out of time. As soon as he arrived in Sparta, Alcibiades used his charm to make himself welcome. He inflamed his Spartan hosts with lurid stories of what would happen if the Athenians conquered Syracuse. He urged them to renew the war by sending troops to the aid of the embattled Syracusans. He also told them to take the war almost directly to Athens itself by building a permanent fortification at Decelea (deh-kuh-LEE-uh), only about fifteen miles from the city. It would disrupt Athenian commerce and represent a constant threat.

Alcibiades told the Spartans that he wasn't really betraying Athens because he had been wrongfully driven out: "I do not consider that I am now attacking a country that is still mine; I am rather trying to recover one that is mine no longer; and the true lover of his country is not he who consents to lose it unjustly rather than attack it, but he who longs for it so much that he will go to all lengths to recover it."[11] In other words, Alcibiades claimed that he was actually doing Athens a favor by telling the Spartans about the city's plans and tactics.

The Spartans sent Gylippus (gy-LIH-pus), one of their best commanders, to Syracuse. Far more resolute than Nicias, he gathered thousands of Sicilians and marched on Syracuse. They soon gained the upper hand.

At this point, Nicias was facing defeat but not catastrophe. He could have chosen to cut his losses and sail home in disgrace. Instead, he asked for reinforcements. More ships and more men from Athens arrived in the spring of 413. An attack involving many of these reinforcements turned into a fiasco. The Athenian situation was becoming desperate, yet Nicias still refused to leave. Gylippus took advantage of the situation and raised thousands of additional troops. The approach of these men finally convinced Nicias to leave.

Thucydides wrote, "The Athenian generals seeing a fresh army come to the aid of the enemy, and that their own circumstances, far from improving, were becoming daily worse, and above all distressed by the sickness of the soldiers, now began to repent of not having departed before; and Nicias no longer offering the same opposition, except by urging that there be no open voting, they gave orders as secretly as possible for all to be prepared to sail out from camp at a given signal."[12]

It is likely that the men didn't need any urging to prepare themselves. The optimism with which they had begun the campaign had long since disappeared. They must have been eager to try to escape a terrible situation and go home.

Nature had other ideas. The army was on the verge of departure when there was an eclipse of the moon.

"Most of the Athenians, deeply impressed by this occurrence, now urged the generals to wait; and Nicias, who was somewhat overaddicted to divination and practices of that kind, refused from that moment even to take the question of departure into consideration, until they had waited the thrice nine days prescribed by the soothsayers,"[13] Thucydides explained.

A statue of Heracles, a Greek hero featured in one of Euripides' plays. Heracles is also known as Hercules, his Roman name.

The delay was fatal. A renewed offensive led by Gylippus cut off any chance of escaping by sea. It forced the Athenians into a headlong retreat, which ended on the banks of the Assinarus River and in the quarries in Syracuse.

Some escaped this dismal fate in an unusual way. "A few were rescued because of their knowledge of Euripides [you-RIH-puh-deez; an Athenian playwright], for it seems that the Sicilians were more devoted to his poetry than any other Greeks living outside the mother country," Plutarch wrote. "They had been given their freedom in return for teaching their masters all they could remember of his works, while others, when they took to flight after the final battle, had been given food and water for reciting some of his lyrics."[14]

Euripides

Euripides was one of three great tragic playwrights who lived in Athens during the fifth century BCE. Aeschylus (ES-kuh-lus) and Sophocles (SAH-fuh-kleez) were the others. According to tradition, Euripides was born in 480 BCE on the same day as the historic Greek naval victory over the invading Persians at Salamis. It is more likely that he was born several years earlier.

Little is known about his personal life. According to some scholars, he was born into a well-to-do family. Others maintain that his parents were relatively poor. There are also some hints that he was a good wrestler who nearly qualified for the Olympics.

One of the central features of Athenian public life was an annual drama festival called the Dionysia (dy-uh-NY-jyuh), which featured a competition among the city's playwrights. Euripides entered the competition for the first time in 455 BCE, but it was well over a decade before he finally won. He received the prize only three more times during his life.

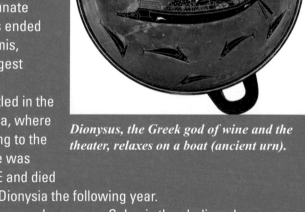

Unlike most of his rivals, he usually wrote about the struggles of everyday people rather than more classical and heroic figures. As classics professor Richmond Lattimore observes, "Though the judges of Dionysus disapproved, there cannot be much doubt that the audience was fascinated."[15]

Euripides wasn't much more fortunate in his personal life. His two marriages ended unhappily. He lived in a cave on Salamis, where he accumulated one of the largest libraries in ancient Athens.

Eventually he left Athens and settled in the northern Greek kingdom of Macedonia, where he composed his final plays. According to the most common version of his death, he was attacked by a pack of dogs in 406 BCE and died

Dionysus, the Greek god of wine and the theater, relaxes on a boat (ancient urn).

of his wounds. Ironically, he won the Dionysia the following year.

In 1997, Greek archaeologists discovered a cave on Salamis they believed was where Euripides had lived for so many years. The chief piece of evidence was a clay pot inscribed with his name.

"I can picture him sitting at the terrace at the entry of the cave, looking out at the Saronic Gulf and composing his plays,"[16] said one of the archaeologists.

Alcibiades returns in triumph to Athens. He had been exiled from the city and sentenced to die a few years earlier for his role in the defeat at Syracuse.

CHAPTER
FIVE

THE END OF THE WAR

Somehow the Athenians managed to rebuild their fleet and continue the war. The conflict had shifted to the Aegean Sea and the Greek colonies in Ionia, the western part of modern-day Turkey. Alcibiades, who wanted to have a hand in the action, fomented anti-Athenian sentiment in the region.

While living in Sparta, he had gained an important enemy: the Spartan king Agis. Alcibiades had a love affair with his wife. Agis fumed at the betrayal and persuaded his fellow Spartans to condemn Alcibiades, who decided to switch his allegiance back to Athens. In 411, he was welcomed on the Athenian-held island of Samos and given a position of leadership. As Thucydides noted, "Alcibiades complained of and deplored his private misfortune in having been banished, and speaking at great length upon public affairs, highly incited [the Athenians'] hopes for the future."[1]

His return was one of the final incidents that Thucydides recorded. His narrative breaks off not long afterward.

He was therefore unable to describe the remarkable resurgence of the Athenians. Just as they had managed to overcome the plague, somehow they also managed to overcome the disaster at Syracuse. One of the primary reasons was Alcibiades. Under his leadership, the Athenians won a stunning naval victory in 410 BCE. Further triumphs sealed his reputation as an outstanding commander. In 407, he finally felt secure

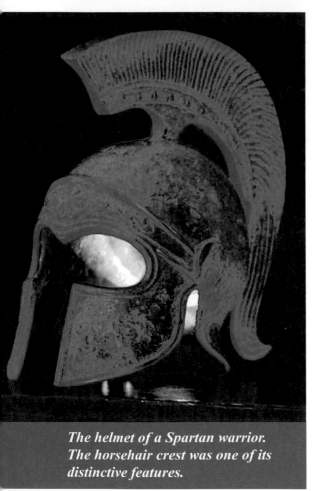

The helmet of a Spartan warrior. The horsehair crest was one of its distinctive features.

enough to return to Athens, even though his death sentence was still technically in force.

He didn't have to worry. "When he landed, people scarcely seemed to have eyes for the other generals they met, but they ran and crowded round Alcibiades, crying out and embracing him," Plutarch writes. "As they escorted him on his way, those who could press near crowned him with garlands."[2]

His triumph was short-lived. The following year, he returned to Ionia. At one point, he left the fleet to join another campaign. He appointed an inexperienced commander and gave him strict orders not to attack the nearby Spartans. Seeing the chance to obtain glory for himself, the commander ignored the orders. He was killed, the Athenians were defeated, and Alcibiades was blamed for the loss. Fearing his reception in Athens, Alcibiades went into exile. He was murdered two years later. There are conflicting accounts of who was responsible, though in all likelihood it was the Spartans.

Later in 406, the Athenian fleet won another significant victory. As Kagan notes, "Once again, Athens ruled the sea and had good reason to hope for survival and even victory in the war."[3]

It was not to be. In the aftermath, it was found that hundreds of men—both living and dead—had been abandoned when a severe storm threatened the fleet. The Athenians put the victorious commanders on trial. They were found guilty and executed, thereby depriving the fleet of their leadership.

They were sorely missed. In 405, the brilliant Spartan general Lysander managed to capture virtually the entire Athenian fleet. With command of the seas, the Spartans could finally deny Athens the steady supply of grain that had helped sustain it for nearly three decades. Facing imminent starvation, Athens had no choice but to surrender. The long and costly war was finally over. No one knows how many people died.

At first, the victorious Spartans wanted to destroy Athens. Instead, the city was allowed to remain in existence. The Long Walls were dismantled, the city became subservient to the Spartans, and the Spartans commandeered the Athenian fleet.

Not surprisingly, there were recriminations in Athens. One result was the execution of Socrates in 399 for his political and religious views. Socrates was executed in 399, which shocked and horrified his disciple Plato.

The era of Spartan domination of Greece was short-lived. Sparta quickly went into decline and suffered a crippling loss to Thebes at the Battle of Leuctra in 371 BCE. The rest of Greece followed two centuries later, when the emerging Roman Republic defeated them at the Battle of Corinth. In 146 BCE, Greece became a Roman province.

Ancient Greek accomplishments in so many fields would live on and remain

In Jacques-Louis David's painting, Socrates prepares to drink the cup of hemlock that will execute him. His crimes included corrupting the youth with his teachings.

important. This was especially true of *History of the Peloponnesian War.* Besides giving a detailed look at the distant past, it also throws light on the major conflicts of the last hundred years.

Victor Davis Hanson notes: "Athens really was like the Germany of World War II, which fought the old European allies of France and

England, took on the vast industrial might of the United States, and tried to invade Soviet Russia."[4]

As he toured the ruins of ancient Syracuse with Thucydides in mind, journalist Robert D. Kaplan wrote, "It was impossible for me not to think of President Lyndon Johnson's dispatching half a million American troops to South Vietnam a decade after President Dwight Eisenhower had sent a small amount of military aid there."[5]

And historian Thomas Cahill observes that the U.S. invasion of Iraq "sent classicists scurrying back to their Thucydides, where they have found frightening parallels between the hubris of seemingly unbeatable Athens—in its fearless resolve to dominate the world even without allies—and the dismissive attitude of the [George W.] Bush administration toward America's traditional friends, toward the UN and its member nations, and toward world opinion."[6]

The Vietnam Veterans Memorial in San Antonio, Texas

Even though Thucydides wrote this passage near the beginning of *History of the Peloponnesian War*, it is perhaps a fitting description of his legacy: "If it [the book] be judged useful by those inquirers who desire an exact knowledge of the past as an aid to the understanding of the future, which in the course of human things must resemble if it does not reflect it, I shall be content. In fine, I have written my work, not as an essay which is to win the applause of the moment, but as a possession for all time."[7]

It seems a virtual certainty that it is indeed a "possession for all time." Thucydides' observations about human nature, human greed, human folly, and human heroism are as valid today as they were when he made them nearly 2,500 years ago.

Socrates and Greek Political Beliefs

Probably born in 470 BCE, Socrates was well into his forties when he fought at the Battle of Delium. Historian Victor Davis Hanson believes that if Socrates had died there, "the entire course of Western philosophical and political thought would have been radically altered."[8]

Socrates didn't die at Delium. After the battle, he became a well-known teacher in Athens who had a great deal of influence on his students. The most famous of these was Plato, who said that he would have become a politician if he hadn't met Socrates. Instead, he became interested in philosophy. He wrote more than two dozen dialogues centered around Socrates.

Plato also became a teacher, and his most famous student was Aristotle (AIR-uh-stah-tul). Many people regard Aristotle as the world's greatest thinker. His beliefs on many subjects, from anatomy to astronomy, were accepted for more than 2,000 years.

Both men wrote extensively about politics. Plato had been horrified when the Athenians executed Socrates. In a plea against democracy, he wrote *The Republic*, which promoted having a committee of rulers after they have had many years of training.

Aristotle studied the governments of 158 Greek poleis. He concluded that there were three forms of government: rule by one man (monarchy), rule by a small group of men (aristocracy), or rule by the people (democracy). Each form had advantages and disadvantages, though he rated democracy the lowest. He thought democracies were too unstable because people could be easily swayed.

He felt that a mixed form of government was best. It would combine the best elements of monarchy, aristocracy, and democracy. The most important thing was keeping a balance among the three.

Socrates, stained glass

The men who drew up the U.S. Constitution in 1787 had studied Aristotle and incorporated many of his ideas. Like the two Greeks, they were suspicious of democracy. Several provisions reflected this suspicion. One was the electoral college, which could overrule the popular vote in electing the president. Another was the U.S. Senate. Senators would be elected by state legislatures rather than by the people. It wasn't until the passage of the Seventeenth Amendment in 1913 that Americans could elect their senators.

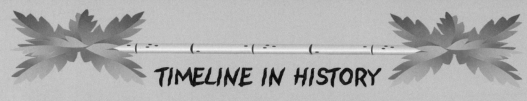

(All dates BCE)

c. 1200 Traditional date of Trojan War.

c. 800 Possible date when Homer composed the *Iliad* and the *Odyssey*.

776 Traditional date for the founding of the Olympic Games.

561 Peisistratus becomes leader of Athens.

550 Cyrus the Great founds the Persian Empire.

507 Athenians establish democracy.

493 Athenian leader Pericles is born.

490 Athenians defeat Persians at the Battle of Marathon.

484 Possible birth date of Herodotus.

480 Invading Persians kill 300 Spartans at the Battle of Thermopylae; combined Greek fleet defeats Persians at the Battle of Salamis; possible birth date of Euripides.

479 Greek victory at Plataea ends Persian invasion.

470 Likely birth date of Socrates.

461 Pericles becomes Athenian leader.

460 Possible birth date of Thucydides; First Peloponnesian War begins.

451 Likely birth date of Alcibiades.

447 Work begins on the Parthenon.

445 Athens and Sparta sign Thirty Years' Treaty, ending the First Peloponnesian War.

436 Democrats in Greek colony of Epidamnus expel their aristocratic rulers.

433 Athenian fleet becomes involved in naval battle between Corcyra and Corinth.

432 Parthenon is completed. Peloponnesian League votes for war with Athens.

431 Peloponnesian War begins. Pericles delivers his Funeral Oration.

430 Plague ravages Athens.

429 Pericles dies.

428 Athenians put down revolt on Mytilene, then vote to kill the men and enslave the women and children; they reconsider the next day.

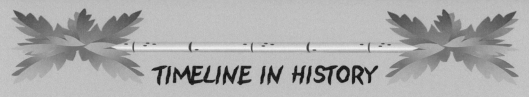

425	Athenians win victory at Sphakteria and hold more than a hundred Spartans as hostages; possible publication date of Herodotus' *Histories*.
424	Boeotians defeat Athenians at the Battle of Delium. Spartans take city of Amphipolis. Possible death date of Herodotus.
423	Thucydides is exiled from Athens.
421	Athens and Sparta agree to the Peace of Nicias; it is supposed to last for 50 years.
418	Spartans win the Battle of Mantinea.
416	Athenians capture the island of Melos; they kill all the men and sell the women and children into slavery.
415	Athenians invade Syracuse but are eventually almost completely annihilated.
411	Alcibiades returns to Athenian side.
410	Athenians win naval victory at Cyzicus.
407	Alcibiades makes triumphant return to Athens.
406	Athenians win naval victory at Arginusae but lose many men; likely death date of Euripides.
405	Spartan general Lysander defeats Athenian fleet at Aegospotami, which cuts off grain supplies.
404	Peloponnesian War ends with Athenian surrender. Alcibiades is killed.
399	The Athenian Assembly finds Socrates guilty of impiety and corrupting the youth; it sentences him to die by drinking hemlock.
397	Possible death date of Thucydides.
371	Spartans are defeated at the Battle of Leuctra.
338	Macedonian King Philip II defeats Greeks at the Battle of Chaeronea.
146	Romans complete their conquest of Greece at the Battle of Corinth, and Greece becomes a Roman province.

CHAPTER NOTES

Chapter 1
Surrender at Syracuse

1. Thucydides, *The Landmark Thucydides*, translated by Richard Crawley, edited by Robert B. Strassler (New York: The Free Press, 1996), p. 477.

2. Ibid.

3. Ibid., p. 478.

4. Ibid., p. 316.

5. Ibid.

6. Ibid., p. 280.

7. Plutarch, *The Rise and Fall of Athens: Nine Greek Lives*, translated by Ian Scott-Kilvert (New York: Penguin Books, 1960), p. 144.

8. Ibid.

9. Herodotus, *The Histories*, translated by Aubrey de Sélincourt (New York: Penguin Books, 1996), p. 307.

Chapter 2
The Prelude to War

1. Thucydides, *The Landmark Thucydides*, translated by Richard Crawley, edited by Robert B. Strassler (New York: The Free Press, 1996), p. 3.

2. Ibid., p. 15.

3. Leo Strauss, *The City and Man* (Chicago: The University of Chicago Press, 1978), p. 158.

4. Ibid.

5. Victor Davis Hanson, "Introduction," in *Thucydides*, p. xii.

6. Ibid.

7. Thucydides, p. 16.

8. Ibid., p. 17.

9. Donald Kagan, *The Peloponnesian War* (New York: Viking, 2003), p. 33.

10. A.R. Burn, *The Pelican History of Greece* (New York: Penguin Books, 1974), p. 260.

11. Plutarch, *Plutarch's Lives: Volume 1*, translated by John Dryden, edited and revised by Arthur Hugh Klough (New York: The Modern Library, 1992), p. 64.

Chapter 3
The Elephant and the Whale

1. Thucydides, *The Landmark Thucydides*, translated by Richard Crawley, edited by Robert B. Strassler (New York: The Free Press, 1996), p. 93.

2. Nigel Bagnall, *The Peloponnesian War: Athens, Sparta, and the Struggle for Greece* (New York: St. Martin's Press, 2004), p. 306.

3. Thucydides, p. 114.

4. Donald Kagan, *The Peloponnesian War* (New York: Viking, 2003), pp. 73–74.

5. Thucydides, p. 119

6. Ibid., p. 118.

7. Ibid., p. 127.

8. James McPherson, "The Art of Abraham Lincoln," *New York Review of Books*, July 16, 1992. http://www.nybooks.com/articles/2852

9. Garry Wills, *Lincoln at Gettysburg: The Words That Remade America* (New York: Simon & Schuster, 1992), p. 44.

10. Ibid., p. 41.

11. Ibid., p. 52.

12. Ibid.

Chapter 4
The Cost of Overconfidence

1. Thucydides, *The Landmark Thucydides*, translated by Richard Crawley, edited by Robert B. Strassler (New York: The Free Press, 1996), p. 254.

2. Victor Davis Hanson, *A War Like No Other: How the Athenians and Spartans Fought the Peloponnesian War* (New York: Random House, 2005), pp. 309–310.

3. Thucydides, p. 327.

4. Ibid., p. 370.

5. Ibid., p. 316.

6. Ibid., p. 357.

7. Plutarch, *Plutarch's Lives: Volume 1*, translated by John Dryden, edited and revised by Arthur Hugh Klough (New York: The Modern Library, 1992), p. 269.

8. Thucydides, p. 361.

9. Ibid., p. 372.

10. Ibid., p. 127.

11. Ibid., p. 415.

12. Ibid., p. 457.

13. Ibid., p. 458.

14. Plutarch, *The Rise and Fall of Athens: Nine Greek Lives*, translated by Ian Scott-Kilvert (New York: Penguin Books, 1960), pp. 242–243.

15. Euripides, *Euripides 1: The Complete Greek Tragedies*, translated by Richmond Lattimore, Rex Warner, Ralph Gladstone, and David Grene; edited by Richmond Lattimore and David Grene (New York: Washington Square Press, 1968), p. vi.

16. "Clay Pot Points to Cave of Euripides," *New York Times*, January 13, 1997. http://query.nytimes.com/gst/fullpage.html?res=9D03E2DC1238F930A25752C0A961958260

Chapter 5
The End of the War

1. Thucydides, *The Landmark Thucydides*, translated by Richard Crawley, edited by Robert B. Strassler (New York: The Free Press, 1996), p. 527.

2. Plutarch, *The Rise and Fall of Athens: Nine Greek Lives*, translated by Ian Scott-Kilvert (New York: Penguin Books, 1960), p. 278.

3. Donald Kagan, *The Peloponnesian War* (New York: Viking, 2003), p. 458.

4. Victor Davis Hanson, *A War Like No Other: How the Athenians and Spartans Fought the Peloponnesian War* (New York: Random House, 2005), p. 311.

5. Robert D. Kaplan, *Mediterranean Winter* (New York: Vintage Books, 2005), p. 101.

6. Thomas Cahill, *Sailing the Wine-Dark Sea: Why the Greeks Matter* (New York: Doubleday, 2003), p. 250.

7. Thucydides, p. 16.

8. Victor Davis Hanson, *Ripples of Battle: How Wars of the Past Still Determine How We Fight, How We Live and How We Think* (New York: Doubleday, 2003), p. 216.

FURTHER READING

For Young Adults

Aird, Hamish. *Pericles: The Rise and Fall of Athenian Democracy.* New York: Rosen Publishing Group, 2003.

Claybourne, Anna. *Ancient Greece.* Chicago: Raintree, 2007.

Doak, Robin S. *Thucydides: Ancient Greek Historian.* Mankato, Minnesota: Compass Point Books, 2006.

Gilbert, Adrian. *Going to War in Ancient Greece.* New York: Franklin Watts, 2000.

Pearson, Anne. *Ancient Greece.* New York: DK Children, 2007.

Whiting, Jim. *Pericles.* Hockessin, Delaware: Mitchell Lane Publishing, 2005.

Works Consulted

Bagnall, Nigel. *The Peloponnesian War: Athens, Sparta, and the Struggle for Greece.* New York: St. Martin's Press, 2004.

Burn, A.R. *The Pelican History of Greece.* New York: Penguin Books, 1974.

Cahill, Thomas. *Sailing the Wine-Dark Sea: Why the Greeks Matter.* New York: Doubleday, 2003.

Cartledge, Paul. *The Spartans: The World of the Warrior-Heroes of Ancient Greece.* Woodstock, New York: The Overlook Press, 2003.

"Clay Pot Points to Cave of Euripides." *New York Times*, January 13, 1997. http://query.nytimes.com/gst/fullpage.html?res=9D03E2DC1238F930A25752C0A961958260

Euripides. *Euripides 1: The Complete Greek Tragedies.* Translated by Richmond Lattimore, Rex Warner, Ralph Gladstone and David Grene. Edited by Richmond Lattimore and David Grene. New York: Washington Square Press, 1968.

Gopnik, Adam. "Angels and Ages: Lincoln's Language and Its Legacy." *New Yorker*, May 28, 2007. http://www.newyorker.com/reporting/2007/05/28/070528fa_fact_gopnik

Hanson, Victor Davis. *Ripples of Battle: How Wars of the Past Still Determine How We Fight, How We Live and How We Think.* New York: Doubleday, 2003.

———. *A War Like No Other: How the Athenians and Spartans Fought the Peloponnesian War.* New York: Random House, 2005.

Herodotus. *The Histories. Translated by Aubrey de Sélincourt.* New York: Penguin Books, 1996.

Kagan, Donald. *The Peloponnesian War.* New York: Viking, 2003.

Kaplan, Robert D. *Mediterranean Winter.* New York: Vintage Books, 2005.

McPherson, James. "The Art of Abraham Lincoln." *New York Review of Books*, July 16, 1992. http://www.nybooks.com/articles/2852

Plutarch. *Plutarch's Lives: Volume 1.* Translated by John Dryden. Edited and revised by Arthur Hugh Klough. New York: The Modern Library, 1992.

Plutarch. *The Rise and Fall of Athens: Nine Greek Lives.* Translated by Ian Scott-Kilvert. New York: Penguin Books, 1960.

Strauss, Leo. *The City and Man.* Chicago: The University of Chicago Press, 1978.

Taplin, Oliver. *Greek Fire: The Influence of Ancient Greece on the Modern World.* New York: Atheneum, 1990.

Thucydides. *The Landmark Thucydides.* Translated by Richard Crawley. Edited by Robert B. Strassler. New York: The Free Press, 1996.

Wills, Garry. *Lincoln at Gettysburg: The Words That Remade America.* New York: Simon & Schuster, 1992.

On the Internet

Hooker, Richard. "Ancient Greece: The Age of Pericles: The Athenian Empire." http://www.wsu.edu/~dee/GREECE/ATHEMP.HTM

Peloponnesian War http://www.historyforkids.org/learn/greeks/history/peloponnesian.htm

Peloponnesian War http://www.socialstudiesforkids.com/wwww/world/peloponnesiandef.htm

Tetlow, Elisabeth M. "The Status of Women in Greek, Roman and Jewish Society." http://www.womenpriests.org/classic/tetlow1.asp

The Women of Athens http://www.mnsu.edu/emuseum/prehistory/aegean/culture/womenofathens.html

archaeologists   (ar-kee-AH-luh-jists)—People who study past civilizations.

classicists   (CLAA-suh-sists)—People who study the literature and history of ancient Greece and Rome.

divination   (dih-vih-NAY-shun)—The study of supernatural events to make predictions.

exile   (EK-zyl)—Force to leave one's native land.

fetid   (FEH-tid)—Having a strong, unpleasant smell.

hubris   (HYOO-bris)—Too much pride or self-confidence.

invincible   (in-VIN-sih-bul)—Not able to be overcome or conquered.

javelins   (JAV-lins)—Lightweight spears that can be thrown a great distance.

naturalistic   (naa-chuh-ruh-LIS-tic)—Having natural causes and explanations.

oration   (or-AY-shun)—A carefully prepared speech presented in a solemn and dignified manner.

poleis   (poh-LAYS)—Plural of *polis*.

polis   (POH-lis)—A Greek city-state, consisting of a central town or city and the surrounding countryside.

protagonists   (pro-TAA-guh-nists)—Leading characters in a play or event.

quoit   (QWOYT)—A flat ring made of rope used in a throwing game.

recriminations   (ree-krih-muh-NAY-shuns)—Accusations.

soothsayers   (SOOTH-say-ers)—People who try to predict the future.

Thucydides

INDEX